¡VIVA MÉXICO!

A Story of Benito Juárez and Cinco de Mayo

By Argentina Palacios

Alex Haley, General Editor

Illustrations by Howard Berelson

STECK-VAUGHN
C O M P A N Y
A Subsidiary of National Education Corporation

To the people of Mexico

Published by Steck-Vaughn Company.

Text, illustrations, and cover art copyright © 1993 by Dialogue Systems, Inc., 627 Broadway, New York, New York 10012. All rights reserved.

Cover art by Howard Berelson

Printed in the United States of America   1 2 3 4 5 6 7 8 9 R 98 97 96 95 94 93 92

Library of Congress Cataloging-in-Publication Data

Palacios, Argentina.
    Viva México!: the story of Benito Juárez and Cinco de Mayo / author, Argentina Palacios; illustrator, Howard Berelson.
        p. cm.—(Stories of America)
    Summary: A biography of the Zapotec Indian who grew up to become the President of Mexico and lead his country in a war for independence.
    ISBN 0-8114-7214-0 (hardcover).—ISBN 0-8114-8054-2 (softcover)
    1. Juárez, Benito, 1806–1872—Juvenile literature. 2. Mexico—History—European intervention, 1861–1867—Juvenile literature. 3. Presidents—Mexico—Biography—Juvenile literature. [1. Juárez, Benito, 1806–1872. 2. Presidents—Mexico. 3. Zapotec Indians—Biography. 4. Indians of Mexico— Biography.] I. Berelson, Howard, ill. II. Title. III. Series.
F1233. J9P35 1993
972'.07'092—dc20
[B]   92–18071
                                                                                          CIP
                                                                                          AC

ISBN 0-8114-7214-0 (Hardcover)
ISBN 0-8114-8054-2 (Softcover)

A Note

from Alex Haley, General Editor

Benito Juárez came forward when his country needed him. And when things looked bad for Mexico, he refused to give up. In Benito Juárez, Mexico found true leadership and true courage.

This is a story of the strong will of one man, and of his love for his country.

High in the mountains of Mexico was a tiny, sun-baked adobe house. Its floors were dirt, and it had almost no furniture. It was a poor house in a poor village.

In one of its two rooms, Josefa and Rosa Juárez waited. Both girls knew that by the end of the day, they would have a new brother or sister. They waited quietly to hear its first cry. Why was the baby taking so long?

Then Josefa and Rosa heard a faint wail. *The baby!* They rushed into Mamá's room. Proudly, she showed them their new brother. How tiny he was!

His eyes were tightly closed. When they opened, they would be dark, dark brown like the girls' eyes.

Mamá and Papá called the baby Benito. They never dreamed that one day all Mexico would know his name.

Although Benito's family gave him a lot of love, they did not have much else to give him.

The Juárez family, like their neighbors, were Zapotec Indians. Few of the Zapotecs spoke Spanish, Mexico's main language. Fewer could read or write. The Zapotecs were so poor that the village had no school.

When Benito was only three, his life changed greatly. Both his parents died. So his grandparents took in the Juárez children. For eight years they raised them. But when Benito was about eleven, his grandparents died. So he went to a nearby village to live with his Uncle Bernardino.

One afternoon, Benito stood in a field by Uncle Bernardino's home. All around him, the sheep nipped at the short grass. Watching his uncle's sheep was one of Benito's jobs.

Benito looked out toward the cornfield. The corn plants were growing tall. Benito could see Uncle Bernardino in the cornfield, pulling up weeds. It was hard work. Soon Benito would help his uncle with the harvest.

Baaa-aa, cried a sheep. Benito turned back to watch the flock. He knew he had to keep his eye on the sheep so none of them would wander away.

Benito wished that his uncle could come over to the field and sit with him. Then Uncle Bernardino could teach him to read better. Uncle Bernardino knew how to read, and he wanted Benito to learn how, too. So whenever he could, Uncle Bernardino taught Benito.

Benito loved to learn. But farm work went on all day. Uncle Bernardino had very little time to teach.

So Benito pretended *he* was a teacher. He taught the sheep what he knew. Sometimes a sheep would raise its head and look at Benito. Ah, a bright pupil! But then it always bent down again and began eating the grass .

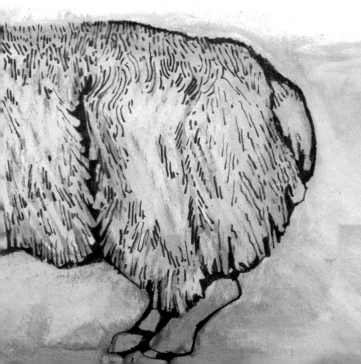

Soon Benito had learned as much as Uncle Bernardino could teach him. To learn more, he would have to go to school. But the nearest schools were in the city of Oaxaca. And that was forty miles away.

Then Benito thought of his sister Josefa. She now worked in Oaxaca. He could stay with her. He knew it would be hard, but he decided to leave his uncle's home. It was the only way he could go to school.

He set out for the city without a horse or a burro to ride. All he had were his strong legs.

Benito walked across miles of rocky fields and over dusty dirt roads. He grew tired and hungry. But he kept going. At last, he saw the city of Oaxaca.

Benito was amazed at his first sight of Oaxaca. Compared to his tiny village of 150 people, it was huge! Everywhere there were large buildings. Some were two floors high, or three, or even more!

And the crowds! Benito couldn't believe the crowds. The streets were full of people. People walking, people running, people in carts, and people on horseback. He did not think there were so many people in the whole world. Yet here they were all in one city.

Benito found his way to the house of the Maza family. His sister Josefa worked as a cook for the Mazas. Josefa was glad to see her little brother. But she could not pay for Benito's schooling. Benito would have to work in order to pay for school.

Benito went to work for a bookbinder who needed a helper. In return, the bookbinder paid for Benito's schooling.

At last Benito could go to a real school. He wished everyone could be as lucky as he was.

Benito went to school for many years. He also studied on his own. He learned reading, writing, history, science, and even law. In 1831, he became a lawyer. He was 25 years old.

As a lawyer, he often took the cases of poor people who could not pay him. They knew they could trust Benito Juárez to do his best.

But Benito Juárez wanted to help even more people. He could not do this just as a lawyer. He decided to work in the government.

Benito Juárez was chosen for many government posts in the state of Oaxaca. Finally, he became the state's governor.

He wanted all children to have a chance to learn to read. So he helped to open more than forty schools in poor villages like his own.

Juárez did many things for the people of Oaxaca. He especially wanted to help Oaxaca's Indians. "I am an Indian and I do not forget my own people," he said.

Many people saw that Benito Juárez was a good governor. They decided that he would be a good President of Mexico. In 1861, Benito Juárez became President of Mexico.

But Juárez became President during a dangerous time. Far away, in France, the French Emperor decided that he would try to take over Mexico. He sent soldiers across the sea to fight the Mexican people. The year was 1862.

The French soldiers thought they would have an easy time in Mexico. They were sure that they were stronger than the Mexican soldiers.

The Mexicans got word that the French army was marching through Mexico. High in the hills, the Mexicans waited for the French troops.

On the morning of *Cinco de Mayo*—May 5—the Mexicans saw the French soldiers reach the city of Puebla.

They saw thousands of French soldiers on horseback. Thousands more marched on foot. The soldiers' rifles stuck up like a forest of prickly spikes. Horses pulled huge, heavy cannon over the bumpy ground.

There were so many weapons and so many soldiers!

The Mexicans knew that the French had a strong army. But the French soldiers looked tired after their long march. The Mexicans began to believe that they had a chance to win.

The two armies got ready to fight.

At about noon the battle began. The French thought the battle would be over quickly. But to their surprise, the Mexicans fought hard and well. After two hours, the armies were still fighting.

The French soldiers saw a weak part in the Mexican line and charged. But a group of Mexican soldiers pushed them back.

By afternoon, the French were running out of bullets and cannon shells. Many soldiers on both sides were dead or wounded. Finally, the French rode away.

The Mexicans had won. *¡Viva México!* Now they knew that they were strong. Now they knew that they had a chance to beat the French.

The French Emperor was angry at the news of the battle of *Cinco de Mayo*. He sent 30,000 more soldiers to Mexico. Soon, they took over Mexico City.

President Juárez had to flee the city. But he waited until the Mexican flag came down from the flagpole. As the flag was lowered, a band played the Mexican national anthem.

President Juárez took the flag in his hands and kissed it. *"¡Viva México!"* he cried. Then Benito Juárez rode away into the hills.

For five years, the French ruled Mexico. But Benito Juárez and the other Mexican leaders kept fighting. Often they had to hide to escape capture, but they never gave up.

At last, in 1867, they won. The French left. Mexico was free again. From that time on, no other country has ever ruled Mexico.

President Juárez rode back into Mexico City. He raised the Mexican flag over the city. *¡Viva México!* he cried.

¡Viva México! ¡Viva Juárez! the people shouted.

Cinco de Mayo

Every country has special holidays. Some holidays celebrate the birthdays of people that helped the country. Some holidays mark important dates in the country's history.

Cinco de Mayo—the Fifth of May—is a holiday that Mexican people celebrate. On this holiday, they remember the battle of Puebla. They remember the brave fighters who won against the armies of France. They honor heroes that helped Mexico become free once more. One of these heroes was Benito Juárez.